INSTRUMENTATION OF THE TAXONOMY OF EDUCATIONAL OBJECTIVES: COGNITIVE DOMAIN

Taxonomy Classification	Key Words	
	Examples of Infinitives	Examples of Direct Objects
1.00 Knowledge		
1.10 Knowledge of Specifics		
1.11 Knowledge of Terminology	to define, to distinguish to acquire, to identify, to recall, to recognize	vocabulary, terms, terminology, meaning(s), definitions, referents, elements
1.12 Knowledge of Specific Facts	to recall, to recognize, to acquire, to identify	facts, factual information, sources, names, dates, events, persons, places, time periods, properties, examples, phenomena
1.20 Knowledge of Ways and Means of Dealing with Specifics		
1.21 Knowledge of Conventions	to recall, to identify, to recognize, to acquire	form(s), conventions, uses, usage, rules, ways, devices, symbols, representations, style(s), format(s)
1.22 Knowledge of Trends Sequences	to recall, to recognize, to acquire, to identify	action(s), processes, movement(s), continuity, development(s), trend(s), sequence(s), causes, relationship(s), forces, influences
1.23 Knowledge of Classifications and Categories	to recall, to recognize, to acquire, to identify	area(s), type(s), feature(s), class(es), set(s), division(s) arrangement(s), classification(s), category/categories
1.24 Knowledge of Criteria	to recall, to recognize, to acquire, to identify	criteria, basics, elements
1.25 Knowledge of Methodology	to recall, to recognize, to acquire, to identify	methods, techniques, approaches, uses, procedures, treatments

Metfessel, N. S., Michael, W. B., and Kirsner, D. A. Instrumentation of Bloom's Krathwol's Taxonomies for Writing of Educational Objectives, *Psychology in the Sc* 6, 1969, pp. 227-231.

INSTRUMENTATION OF THE TAXONOMY OF EDUCATIONAL OBJECTIVES: COGNITIVE DOMAIN

Taxonomy Classification	Key Words Examples of Infinitives	Examples of Direct Objects
1.30 Knowledge of the Universals and Abstractions in a Field		
1.31 Knowledge of Principles, Generalizations	to recall, to recognize, to acquire, to identify	principle(s), generalization(s), proposition(s), fundamentals, laws, principal elements, implication(s)
1.32 Knowledge of Theories and Structures	to recall, to recognize, to acquire, to identify	theories, bases, interrelations, structure(s), organization(s), formulation(s)
2.00 Comprehension		
2.10 Translation	to translate, to transform, to give in own words, to illustrate, to prepare, to read, to represent, to change, to rephrase, to restate	meaning(s), sample(s), definitions, abstractions, representations, words, phrases
2.20 Interpretation	to interpret, to reorder, to rearrange, to differ to differentiate, to distinguish, to make, to draw, to explain, to demonstrate	relevancies, relationships, essentials, aspects, new view(s), qualifications, conclusions, methods, theories, abstractions
2.30 Extrapolation	to estimate, to infer, to conclude, to predict, to differentiate, to determine, to extend, to interpolate, to extrapolate, to fill in, to draw	consequences, implications, conclusions, factors, ramifications, meanings, corollaries, effects, probabilities

2320

Writing Behavioral Objectives

THE BURGESS EDUCATIONAL PSYCHOLOGY SERIES FOR THE TEACHER
Consulting Editor: John F. Feldhusen, Purdue University

Writing
Behavioral
Objectives

A Guide to
Planning Instruction

William J. Kryspin
John F. Feldhusen
Purdue University

Foreword by Charles E. Kline
Purdue University

BURGESS PUBLISHING COMPANY · MINNEAPOLIS, MINNESOTA

2   3   4   5   6   7   8   9   0

1/29/76 *Beckert Taylor* 3.95

Foreword

This is a programmed text for students of education, particularly those learning to become teachers. The authors have focused upon behavioral objectives in such a way that the learner is guided through a sequential series of learning stages, from distinguishing among objectives to using a specification chart as a guide to writing objectives. The content and programming have been shaped by proven effectiveness, and they emphasize that learning must be a successful and rewarding experience for the student.

Part I develops a conceptual framework for writing behavioral objectives. Part II establishes the linkage between the cognitive domain and behavioral objectives. Part III carries the learner forward to analyzing and organizing subject matter according to behavioral objective perspective and to writing objectives at different and appropriate cognitive levels.

The material in this text is not a panacea, nor is it a magic potion; rather it is a framework for sound, concentrated learning relative to effective instruction.

September, 1973

Charles E. Kline
Department of Education
Purdue University

Student's Preface

For some of you this may be your first experience with programmed or self-instructional material. Notice the emphasis on "self"! You supply the drive. This should not be too great a task for many of you. And, hopefully, you will enjoy the following advantages of this type of instruction:

- You have the opportunity to proceed at your own learning rate.
- You can use this unit anywhere—well, almost anywhere!
- You will receive immediate confirmation or feedback on what you do.
- You have the chance to go back over the material you might be unsure of.
- You will have to think—sometimes very hard!
- You will be able to make mistakes—even stupid ones—and to correct yourself. You're in the driver's seat!
- You will receive personal attention from the instructor at various points throughout the unit.

But, what do you *do* in this kind of unit? Well, part of your activity will be reading, thinking, writing, decision making, chuckling (hopefully), talking, explaining, and memorizing (not much). Rather than spin your wheels talking about what you're going to do, why not get started. Turn to the introduction on page 1.

Purdue University

William J. Kryspin
John W. Feldhusen

Contents

Writing Behavioral Objectives

Introduction

With the ever increasing need for continuing learning in our society, it becomes imperative that school learning must be a successful and rewarding experience *for the student*. Note that the learning encounter should be student-centered. Granted, most teachers are concerned with the fact that students learn something, but many teachers are more vitally concerned with surviving that English class period, or the morning session, or until Friday, or until vacation, or with just providing the student with some kind of activity that will keep him interested.

The present unit is both student-centered and teacher-oriented. How, you ask, can one unit accomplish a feat that few teachers have been able to master? In the main, the answer will become quite apparent as you progress through the unit. You might ponder if indeed there is any real obstacle that prevents teaching from being genuinely involved with students and an enjoyable encounter for teachers.

Consider for the moment a boy scout troop meandering through the woods. What happens if the troop leader has no sense of direction or no planned route to follow? Obviously, you say, the troop probably will have difficulty reaching its destination. Perhaps the troop members will become disgruntled and disenchanted with hiking. Moreover, the troop leader may become overly anxious at the prospect of being lost in the woods with the now "unfriendly natives." While these outcomes are all probable, the scout leader can readily circumvent them by specifying at the outset of the hike where they are going.

By now you are asking, "What kind of a unit is this that talks about boy scouts and survival?" In practice, many teachers face problems similar to those of the troop leader. Unfortunately for most teachers, one of the hardest tasks is that of specifying what it is that the kids are supposed to learn in their classes. Most teachers can think of things to do in class, such as lead discussions, show films, lecture, etc., and most teachers can write a test of some kind, but the teaching activities and the tests may not be related at all to what the teacher and/or the students consider really worthwhile learning. Specifying really worth-

1

while learning in such a way that it is useful to the teacher and to the student is *the* problem.

But before you venture too far into the woods, it seems desirable to pause long enough to specify what you should learn from this unit, or, if you prefer, what your final destination is. The following objectives denote rather explicitly what you are expected to learn. In addition, they represent models of objectives like the ones you should be able to write when you have finished this unit.

As a student who has completed this unit, you will be able to:

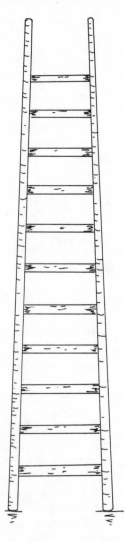

(11) Use a specification chart (or blueprint) as a guide to writing objectives.

(10) Write objectives at each of the six levels of the taxonomy in the subject area of your choice.

(9) Specify according to the Cognitive Taxonomy the level of a given educational objective.

(8) List the six basic levels of the cognitive domain.

(7) Judge the adequacy of a component in an objective according to the criteria denoted in this unit.

(6) Analyze a given educational objective by identifying the components.

(5) Write objectives that embody all the components of a good behavioral objective for one approach.

(4) Relate behavioral objectives to instructional and testing activities in your own words.

(3) Identify all the components of a well-stated behavioral objective.

(2) Translate instructional objectives into student-centered behavioral objectives.

(1) Distinguish between specific educational objectives that are student-centered and other types of objectives when shown examples of each.

At this point you may be thinking, "How can I remember all these things to earn, much less learn them?" Take heart! Look at this unit as though you were climbing a ladder. The objectives for this unit were stated in reverse order to simulate climbing a ladder. Once you finish one objective, you're one step higher, and hopefully you won't have to go back and "climb" the objectives you've already mastered.

However, before you start climbing, please read the title on the next page. If it seems to fit you, start reading there. If it does not apply to you, go on to page

I Do Not Plan to Teach on the Elementary, Secondary or College Level

In several sections of this unit you will be asked to write some objective based on subject matter in the area and grade level at which you hope to teach. For most students taking a course in which this unit is used, this will not be too difficult a task because they have had enough experience in classrooms or in courses in their major field to have a fair knowledge of the required subject matter. But a few students have a handicap. Sometimes, there are student nurses, physical therapists, prospective counselors, and remedial specialists using the unit who do not intend to be classroom teachers and cannot easily identify a subject matter area or grade level.

Several alternatives are suggested for students handicapped in this manner. One alternative is to select subject matter from some area in which they have had several college level courses. A prospective nurse will have had several courses in biology from which she can draw. She could go back and use her text and subject matter from biology courses. Secondly, a student might consider dropping back to the high school or elementary level for subject matter which he may remember well. For example, he may have been strong in the sciences in high school and may be able to drop back to chemistry for his subject matter area. Thirdly, a student may find himself among numerous people in non-teaching areas who may, nevertheless, have responsibilities to teach individuals or small groups. The counselor may have to teach the teachers in his school something about testing procedures. The remedial teacher has to teach reading skills to individual children. Or, if you are a speech therapist, you might be requested to conduct in-service training sessions for teachers. Thus, students in these areas can find subject matter and appropriate grade level for the exercises required in this text. Perhaps your interests will suggest still other alternatives.

Turn now to page 6.

Part I

What Are Objectives?

MOST IF NOT ALL of you have been exposed to the term *objective* in the past. Often, military or political aims are referred to as objectives. For example, the President has as an objective—"the stabilization of the inflationary spiral." You may have graduating from college as an objective. Another way of describing these general aims is to refer to them as goals. Typically, goals are defined as aims or objects toward which an individual or a group strive with an apparent or underlying purpose that directs what the person or the group does. The basic aspects of any goal are: (a) an aim and (b) purposive activity. Often, goals can be stated only in general terms because the aims may be very broad in nature and the underlying philosophy or guiding principles are complex and cannot be readily or succinctly spelled out.

Certainly, you will agree that education, as any purposeful activity, has many broad goals. For example, colleges and universities might have as a goal:

> To provide students with the opportunity to become competent in a field of endeavor suitable to their abilities and needs.

Another educational goal related to this unit in particular might be broadly stated as:

> To promote competency in teaching.

While goals provide a general tenor or frame of reference, they are not specific enough for directing the activities of a teacher of an ancient history course or a student in English composition. What the student and teacher both need are explicit statements or objectives of what a particular course or unit has as its expected outcome. Therefore, a *specific educational objective* might be defined as a form of written communication that tells the reader *exactly* what the writer *intends to accomplish*. Another way of characterizing a specific educational objective is to say that it must state *observable* and *measurable behavior*. Hence, the term often applied to specific educational objectives is behavioral objectives. The adjective "observable" is used to ensure that the behavior specified is something that anyone can see, since, obviously, it is extremely difficult to measure the invisible.

Nonsense, you say! This is just some more educational jargon! Okay! Try the following experiment:

Take a deep breath. Hold it. Now open your mouth and exhale. Can you tell how wide the column of air was? How far from your mouth was the air propelled? How could you measure it? Could someone else measure it?

Unless the room you're in is quite chilly, you probably could not see your breath and consequently couldn't measure it either. However, if the temperature is sufficiently low, the escaping air forms a miniature cloud of water vapor that is visible and therefore measurable.

The second adjective "measurable" is essential so that you can tell whethe the objective has been achieved or whether more effort is still needed. Mor will be said about measurability and observability later in this unit.

Use of the term "behavior" does not mean merely physical movement actions, or motor behavior. In school settings, the term refers generally t some form of verbal behavior, although motor behavior may be of importanc in such school subjects as physical education, industrial arts, home economic and art. However, much of the time when reference is made to behavior objectives, the intended meaning is verbal behavioral objectives. For exampl here is a behavioral objective which really involves verbal behavior:

> The pupil will be able to describe the essential characteristics of a steam engine.

To describe undoubtedly refers to some verbal behavior which may be writte or oral.

In some cases, a behavioral objective may include a specification of a produc which results from the student's behavior. The teacher might examine the pro duct to decide if the student has learned what the teacher wanted to teach him For instance, consider the behavioral objective:

> The student will be able to write a five line poem in iambic pentameter on the subject of his choice.

Certainly, the teacher will probably not want to watch (even if possible each student perform this writing task. The teacher is interested in examinin the product of the student's efforts when he is finished. From the finishe poem, the teacher can judge whether or not the objective has been attained.

Look at page 9 now to check yourself.

In terms of the characteristics of a behavioral objective, indicate by checking the appropriate box whether or not you consider the following objectives to be adequate.

1. The students will really understand the major causes of the Civil War.

[ ] Adequate   [ ] Inadequate

2. The pupils will be able to print the letters of the alphabet when pronounced by the teacher.

[ ] Adequate   [ ] Inadequate

3. The students will be able to list three characteristics of an acid.

[ ] Adequate   [ ] Inadequate

4. The pupils will be able to appreciate the value of music.

[ ] Adequate   [ ] Inadequate

Turn to page 10 to check your answers.

Answers

1. Inadequate

2. Adequate

3. Adequate

4. Inadequate

If you got them all right, HOORAY!!!   Turn to page 13.
If you missed item 1 or 4, look at page 11.
If you missed item 2 or 3, turn to page 12.

How do you *see* understanding? Is it blue? Colorless? Maybe pink and short? Tall and black? To be an adequate behavioral objective, the behavior must be *observable*. Don't be fooled by "able to appreciate" either! You can't observe the act of appreciating. Remember, if it isn't observable behavior, it is not a good behavioral objective.

Now turn to page 13.

Aren't printing and listing observable behaviors? You certainly can judge whether this is a "B" or an "E." Your pencil must have slipped. Watch it!

Go on to the next page.

By now you may have an inkling as to why behavioral objectives, rather than broad goals, are needed to determine whether your aims in teaching are being met. It is important that you are able to distinguish behavioral objectives from broad goals. (Recall the first objective stated on page 2.)

Consider the following statements:

Broad Goal	*Behavioral Objective*
Develop an understanding of the Pythagorean theorem.	Be able to solve for the length of a side of a triangle using the Pythagorean theorem.

Look at the broad goal first. What is the behavior? Maybe it's "develop" or maybe it's "understanding." But in either case, it's surely not observable. You can't pry open the lid on a student's head and look inside and see him understanding or developing. Moreover, it does not specify behavior that is measurable. Note the generality with which the broad goal is stated. This goal is so broad that it could apply to both student and teacher.

Now look at the behavioral objective. The behavior expected of the student is clearly "to solve for the length of a side of a triangle." If you were so inclined, you could peer over a student's shoulder and watch him solve the problem. Moreover, you can measure or determine by looking at the method and the answer if the student has learned the task intended. It should be clear to you what to look for in distinguishing between behavioral objectives and broad goals. Goals are usually stated in rather vague terms encompassing the more global outcomes of educational endeavor in various subject matter areas. In contrast, behavioral objectives define specific student performance resulting from instruction in a particular subject. If you don't feel it is clear, you might want to put this unit down and read pages I-6 through I-16 in the CORD Manual edited by Jack Crawford, 1969. Note: This manual may be available in the school's library. If not, you can purchase your own copy by writing to:

Teaching Research Division
Oregon State System of Higher Education
Oregon College of Education Campus
Monmouth, Oregon 97361

Otherwise, turn to page 14.

Pop Quiz!

Determine which of the following are behavioral objectives and which are broad goals by checking the appropriate box. For those you check as behavioral objectives, *underline* the behavior required of the student.

1. The pupil will be able to draw and label the parts of a right triangle.

    [   ] Goal   [   ] Behavioral Objective

2. The pupil will develop an understanding of the Uncertainty Principle.

    [   ] Goal   [   ] Behavioral Objective

3. The student will be able to describe the economic policy of laissez-faire in his own words.

    [   ] Goal   [   ] Behavioral Objective

4. The student will be able to name all the major components of a dress pattern when shown a miniature one.

    [   ] Goal   [   ] Behavioral Objective

5. The student will attain competence as a reader.

    [   ] Goal   [   ] Behavioral Objective

Turn to page 16 to check your answers.

Another important aspect of behavioral objectives that has been implied so far is that while they may be beneficial to the teacher, they are *primarily student-centered*. They tell the student how he or she is expected to perform (behave) after completing the unit of instruction. It is necessary, therefore, that the behavior specified in the objective be that of the student after you have taught him something.

Consider the following examples of objectives:

Objective A	*Objective B*
Prepare slides to show the students the differences between igneous, sedimentary, and metamorphic rock.	Be able to differentiate the three types of rock when given samples of each.

Notice in Objective A that the behavior specified refers to what the teacher is going to do. Objectives of this type are often referred to as instructional objectives because they tell what activities a teacher performs. No mention is made of what is expected of the student. While behavior is implied on the part of the students, you certainly could not classify the behavior as stemming from your teaching activity. The ability to see is generally assumed to be a natural activity rather than a learned activity. Hence Objective A would be classified as an instructional objective rather than a student-centered behavioral objective.

In Objective B, the *students* are expected to differentiate the types of rock. This objective specifies something the *student* will be able to do after he has been taught. It would be considered a student-centered behavioral objective. From now on in this unit the term *behavioral objective* will always imply student-centeredness.

So far you have seen examples of goals, instructional objectives, and behavioral objectives. You may have heard or surely will hear of many other types of objectives, such as planning objectives, informational objectives, enabling objectives, operational objectives, and terminal objectives, to name a few. The list seems endless! However, for the purposes of this unit, only a clear understanding of the differences between goals, instructional objectives, and behavioral objectives will be required.

Turn to page 17.

Answers

1. Behavioral Objective   <u>to draw and label</u>
2. Goal
3. Behavioral Objective   <u>to describe</u>
4. Behavioral Objective   <u>to name</u>
5. Goal

If you got them all right, EXCELLENT! Go back to page 15.
If you missed one, reread page 13, then go back to page 15.
If you missed more than one, STOP!!! Pick up the CORD Manual and read pages I-6 through I-16. Then turn back to page 15.

Now you get to try your hand at something more difficult. Listed below are several statements which may be goals, instructional objectives, or behavioral objectives. On the line preceding each statement, indicate by letter (G = goal, I = instructional objective, and B = behavioral objective) what each statement is. For those you mark B, underline the behavior.

_____ 1. The student will be able to run the 100/yard dash in under 15 seconds.

_____ 2. The students will be shown a film that describes the symptoms of venereal diseases.

_____ 3. The pupils will be able to analyze a poem according to its meter, measure, and form.

_____ 4. The students will develop skills necessary for employment in business.

_____ 5. The pupils will be assembled for group discussion on the causes of the Civil War.

_____ 6. The students will be given a demonstration on the use of carbon tetrachloride as a cleaning agent.

_____ 7. The pupils will be able to state the major causes of heart disease in the United States.

_____ 8. The students will learn self-discipline.

_____ 9. The students will be able to apply Einstein's theory of relativity to sub-atomic structures.

_____ 10. The students will become good citizens.

Turn to page 18 to check your answers.

Answers

1. B   to run

2. I

3. B   to analyze

4. G

5. I

6. I

7. B   to state

8. G

9. B   to apply

10. G

If you got all the items right, skip ahead to page 21.
If you missed any of these items (4, 8, or 10), go immediately to page 19.
If you missed any of these items (1, 3, 7, or 9), go to page 20.
If you missed any of these items (2, 5, or 6), go to page 21.

If you have already read the CORD Manual (pages I-6 through I-16), please find your instructor. Then yell, "HELP!!!"

Otherwise, read the CORD Manual pages I-6 through I-16. Then turn to page 17 and try the exercises again.

Note that in each of the items, 1, 3, 7, and 9, the behaviors "to run," "to analyze," "to state," and "to apply" are all observable behaviors that are performed by the student. In each case there results a measurable outcome directly related to the student's behavior. Thus, each of these are clearly student-centered behavioral objectives.

If you are still unclear, reread pages 6 through 8.   Then proceed to page 21. If you think you've got it, then go directly to page 21.

Perhaps the relationship between instructional objectives and behavioral objectives is still unclear to you. To clarify the distinction, recall that behavioral objectives are student-centered (i.e., they specify actions the student will be able to perform). Instructional objectives, on the other hand, refer to things the *teacher* does or to the way the *teacher* acts toward the student in order to guide him more assuredly to the attainment of the behavioral objectives.

Here are some teacher actions that serve to help children:

— The teacher shows the student how to use a microscope.
— The teacher gives the student special exercises in diagramming sentences.
— The students will be shown a film on the causes of the Civil War.
— The teacher demonstrates the classical ballet forms.
— The students will be assigned to debate teams for discussion of foreign policy.
— The teacher describes plant transpiration.

For each of these teacher actions or instructional objectives, there is a corresponding behavioral objective for the student. For the first one, it could be:

The student will be able to operate a microscope when given prepared slides.

The second one might be:

The student will be able to correctly diagram sentences when given complex sentences.

Now it's your turn. For each of the remaining instructional objectives given on page 21, formulate a behavioral objective.

_____

_____

_____

_____

_____

_____

_____

_____

_____

_____

_____

After you have finished look on page 24 for models of the corresponding behavioral objectives.

In closing this section, it is well to point out that much of the time teaching actions involve the following general functions:

1. Presenting information to pupils.
2. Giving a verbal description of how to perform a skill.
3. Showing how to perform a skill.
4. Directing students in trying to perform a skill.
5. Supervising student trials and providing feedback to help correct them.
6. Providing reinforcement or encouragement when correct behaviors occur.
7. Setting up or staging problem situations in which students must discover solutions.

These general teaching actions are closely related to behavioral objectives. When a teacher has behavioral objectives to guide her in teaching, the task of selecting worthwhile teaching activities is much easier. And if students are informed of the objectives, their motivation to achieve will be increased considerably. Much of the lack of student motivation in many classes stems from the failure of both teachers and students to know what they are really trying to reach. In a sense, behavioral objectives provide a path out of the woods.

Turn to page 25.

Models of Behavioral Objectives

The students will be able to list the causes of the Civil War.

Or,

The students will be able to state in their own words the causes of the Civil War.

The students will be able to perform the classical ballet forms.

The students will be able to debate the current foreign policy in Israel.

The student will be able to describe in his own words transpiration in plants.

If your behavioral objectives are similar (i.e., they are student-centered and reflect observable behavior), then go back to page 23.

If you feel that yours do not measure up, then get in touch with your instructor.

How to Compose a Behavioral Objective

SURPRISE! YOU HAVE ALREADY "climbed" the first two rungs of the objective ladder for this unit. Now that you can differentiate behavioral objectives from instructional objectives and goals, the next step you will take is learning how to write a *well-stated* behavioral objective. This task is similar to identifying the major parts of a sentence. Many schemes have been devised for this purpose. While the most prominent is still Mager's approach, several authors have developed similar schemes for writing well-stated objectives. You will become acquainted with three approaches to writing behavioral objectives.

The first of these is that of Robert Mager, who set forth his ideas on the subject in a small book entitled *Preparing Instructional Objectives* (1962). Don't let the title confuse you! He is really concerned with writing student-centered behavioral objectives. You might like the entertaining style of Mager's programmed instruction. The book can be read easily within an hour. One drawback to Mager's book, however, is that it does not relate very well to the subject matter you will be teaching in the schools. But the *choice* is yours! You may wish to read Mager only. Feel free to do so! The book should be on the shelf next to you. When you finish Mager, return to this unit on page 41.

Another approach has been devised by Kibler, Barker, and Miles (1970) who define five components in contrast to Mager's three components. If you would prefer their scheme, you may read pages 31 to 43 and 77 to 91 in *Behavioral Objectives and Instruction*. If you choose Kibler, Barker, and Miles, return to this unit on page 41 after you finish reading the pages in their book. The third approach stems from the CORD Manual edited by Jack Crawford (1969). Some of you are already familiar with this manual. The authors of the CORD Manual have devised a clever mnemonic device for remembering the basic components of a well-stated behavioral objective. You will be exposed to their ABCD method in the remainder of this section, although a comparison will be made with Kibler, Barker, and Miles and with Mager at the end of this section in order for you to see the similarity of the approaches.

Stop for a moment! Think of some important components of a behavioral
objective. List your ideas or components below.

_____

_____

_____

_____

_____

Now turn to page 28.

According to the authors of the CORD Manual, there are four basic components to a well-stated behavioral objective to which they attach the mnemonic ABCD. The first component, "A," is *audience*. This part corresponds to the subject in a sentence. It tells the reader *who* is expected to perform the desired behavior. Consider the example:

The students will be able to draw a Venn diagram showing the relationship among events.

Who is expected to draw a Venn diagram? "The students," you say! Right! But which students? All students? Students in home economics? Maybe nursing students? Admit it, you're not sure. The *audience* component in this example is too general. *It must be stated in terms most relevant to the teaching task at hand.* That is, you must narrow it down to those students who are expected to achieve whatever behavior you are trying to teach. Thus, if you want the girls in tenth grade home economics to be able to hem a skirt, the audience component of your objective might be:

The girls in tenth grade home economics will be able to hem a skirt.
AUDIENCE COMPONENT

Although it is important to include sufficient information, you must be careful not to include too many descriptive terms. Use common sense and good judgment in spelling out the important characteristics of the students you are teaching.

Now turn to page 29 for some practice.

Compare your components with these:

1. Subject component—who is performing or learning?

2. Behavior component—what the subject *does*—remember it must be observable!

3. Condition component—when is the student supposed to perform—in what setting, under what conditions?

4. Criterion component—how much or how well is the student expected to perform?

5. Product component—what did the student produce—a list, an essay, a poem, etc.

How well did you do? If you got two or more, give yourself some praise. You're doing GREAT! You should have gotten at least one right from the cue word "behavioral."

Now turn back to page 27.

Try identifying the audience in the following objectives. Underline the "A" component and indicate whether it is well-stated or not. That is, does it contain sufficient relevant descriptors or not?

1. The students will be able to write nine complete sentences.

   ☐ Sufficient   ☐ Insufficient

2. The third grade students with average reading ability will be able to read aloud selected essays.

   ☐ Sufficient   ☐ Insufficient

3. The juniors will be able to sing the school fight song during the basketball games.

   ☐ Sufficient   ☐ Insufficient

4. The twelfth grade males in physical education will be able to run the mile in less than seven minutes.

   ☐ Sufficient   ☐ Insufficient

5. Describe the "audience component" for three of your current courses:

   (a) _____

   (b) _____

   (c) _____

Turn to page 30 to check your answers.

Answers

1. The students—insufficient.

2. The third grade students with average reading ability—sufficient.

3. The juniors—sufficient—you may disagree and prefer to specify who will sing the song more precisely—OK!

4. The twelfth grade males in physical education—sufficient.

5. Students in CS210—speech and hearing students in AU210—students in Biology 108—or any similar description of an audience component in your courses is fine!

If you couldn't identify the audience components of these objectives, STOP!!! Pull out the CORD Manual and read page I-17. Then look at page 31 of this unit.

If you could identify them, TERRIFIC! Go directly to page 31.

The next component you are probably most familiar with by now. It is the "B" or behavioral component. This represents the verb in the sentence. As you might infer from the unit title, *behavior is perhaps the most crucial element* in a well-stated behavioral objective. When you learned to differentiate behavioral objectives from other objectives, you learned that the behavior was *observable* and *measurable*. This means that the verb you select for your behavioral objective must denote some visible activity on the part of the student as a result of your teaching. Some verbs denote readily observable actions, while others do not. For instance, it is impossible to see understanding, knowing, appreciating, believing, or thinking take place in the student. These are not good verbs for behavioral objectives. On the other hand, it is readily observable behavior when the student writes, lists, names, diagrams, plans, draws, points out, etc. Several authors have listed verbs appropriate to various levels of learning (more will be said about this later). See Kibler, Barker, and Miles (1970), pp. 180-184; Mager (1962), p.11; Bloom (1956), Part II; and CORD (1969), p. I-18.

When the action the student is expected to perform after he has learned something is behaviorally stated, the teacher is guided in planning the instruction; the student is directed to learning activity that is relevant; and both the student and the teacher know what form the evaluation process should take.

For example, consider the following objective:

The tenth grade geometry students will be able to solve for the length of a side of a right triangle.   BEHAVIOR

Note that the audience is sufficiently described. But more important, the behavior ("to solve") is a clearly observable activity that results from teaching. The teacher would be aware that the instruction should be directed toward helping the students solve problems; the students would know what is expected of them; and both parties would be alerted to possible test questions (e.g., solve for the hypotenuse of a right triangle given a = 6, b = 4). Again, note that the behavior itself might not be of primary interest as you saw in the example of writing the poem. But the product of interest results from the appropriate behavior specified in the objective.

Turn to page 32 for practice exercises on the behavioral component.

Here are some objectives. Underline the behavior component. Then, indicate whether or not it is a good action verb (observable).

1. The third grade students will be able to understand the Venn diagram.

    [   ]   Observable   [   ]   Not observable

2. The geometry students will be able to demonstrate a proof of S.S.S.

    [   ]   Observable   [   ]   Not observable

3. The fourth grade students will be able to spell aloud the ten words ending in "gh."

    [   ]   Observable   [   ]   Not observable

4. The seniors in civics will be able to prepare a plan for automobile pollution control.

    [   ]   Observable   [   ]   Not observable

5. List three observable behaviors that students might be expected to exhibit after being instructed on the Battle of Vicksburg.

   (a) _____

   (b) _____

   (c) _____

Turn to page 34 to check your answers.

Wow!

You're really moving along. Now you must concentrate on the *conditions* of a well-stated objective. This is the "C" component in the mnemonic. It is important to the student to know what conditions he will be tested under. Often, you may have asked your instructor, "Will it be an open book test?" What you are seeking is *knowledge of the conditions* under which you will be tested. A "yes" to the above question tells you that you will not have to rely on your memory. Another familiar condition is often the time element involved. These instances point to the fact that *conditions are related to the evaluation process*. Since it is not fair to expect students to behave in ways in which they have not been taught to behave, it seems eminently unfair to test under conditions grossly different from those under which the learning took place. Therefore, the conditions stated in the behavioral objective should serve to guide the teacher in planning instruction and in formulating tests. Consider again the example:

Using the Pythagorean theorem, the tenth grade geometry students will be able to solve for the length of the hypotenuse.

Suppose a teacher followed this objective in her instruction, but each time she needed the square root of a number she looked it up in a book of tables. When test time rolled around, the students did not get to use the tables. Obviously "unfair!" you say. True enough. Either the teacher should have provided tables, or she should have modified the objective and her instruction possibly as follows:

Using the Pythagorean theorem and a set of tables, the tenth grade geometry students will be able to solve for the length of the hypotenuse. (Modified objective.)

Or

Using the Pythagorean theorem and without the use of tables, the tenth grade geometry students will be able to solve for the length of the hypotenuse. (Teacher modifies instruction to accommodate lack of tables.)

Now turn to page 35.

Answers

1. to understand—not observable.

2. to demonstrate—observable.

3. to spell—observable.

4. to prepare—observable

5. ... list generals ... / ... give the date ... / ... explain in your own words the outcome ... / ... name two important factors in deciding the outcome ... (if the behavior you specified is observable, you're on the right track.)

If you did not miss any or missed only one, go back to page 33.

If you missed two or more, why not reread pages 35-36, or Chapter 4 of Mager's book? Then, go back to page 33 in this unit.

The description of the conditions should remove any ambiguity in what is expected of the students. Sometimes, the conditions are very easy to state, as in this example:

The fifth grade students will be able to spell five words aloud after the teacher pronounces them.
                         CONDITION COMPONENT

Or, in this example:

Given five sentences, the sixth grade pupils will be able to correctly place
CONDITION COMPONENT
the apostrophe.

However, certain situations involve complex conditions that delimit the performance arena and the transfer of behavior to real life settings. Consider the example:

The senior chemistry student will be able to perform the bromide experiment when he is given one hour, no manuals, an array of chemicals to choose from, and raw glassware to be formed as needed.

Certainly, this objective, while it may be well-stated from the ABC standpoint, is very limited by the conditions. Students in real life will probably not be expected to perform under these conditions. This example points up another aspect to be aware of when imposing conditions. Since it is generally assumed that knowledge that has a broad range of applicability will more likely be frequently used, it probably will be retained longer. To this end, it would be beneficial if the desired behavior were exercised under conditions that could be generalized to many real life situations. This direction of behavior to real life has many implications for the instructional methods and materials currently in use. Suffice it to say at this point that as a guideline the conditional component should reflect the testing situation in all *necessary* aspects. If time is not an important facet of the task to be performed, it should not be included in the conditions.

Turn to page 36 for some exercises on the condition component.

Now it's your chance to analyze some behavioral objectives. Underline th condition component in each objective below and indicate whether it ha applicability to real life or not.

1. The second grade students will be able to identify the words beginning with given letter when they are confronted with pictures of several objects.

   [　] Like real life   [　] Not like real life

2. The students in tenth grade home economics will be able to make a dress i one hour when they are given a choice of patterns and material.

   [　] Like real life   [　] Not like real life

3. The students in third grade math will be able to solve change-making pro blems for items costing more than a dollar.

   [　] Like real life   [　] Not like real life

4. Pupils in eighth grade will be able to explain without using notes the life cycl of an annual plant to the class.

   [　] Like real life   [　] Not like real life

5. You are going to teach a unit on polygons in geometry. Add a "conditio component" to the following objective: "The geometry student will be ab to classify polygons . . . "

_____

Turn to page 38 to check your answers.

The last component of a well-stated behavioral objective to be considered is that of *degree*, "D." *Degree* refers to the level or criterion of acceptable performance for the particular learning task. It forms the decision point about which you decide either that the student has mastered the material sufficiently to go on to the next objective or that more effort is required on this task. As with the other components, the degree aspect guides your effort as well as that of the student. It allows you to exercise your professional judgment regarding the relationship of learning activities. You determine what level of mastery is needed before the next concept or skill can be successfully taught.

Here are some examples of the degree component which specifies the criterion level of acceptable performance:

Given a newspaper account of a political rally, the eigth grade pupil will be able to point out at least half of the instances in which the writer's biases are revealed.

The eleventh grade student will be able to identify all of the instances of alliteration in a sonnet which he has not seen before.

When given a list of 50 spelling words orally, the fourth grade student will be able to write the correct spelling of at least 40 words.

Look back at the third example. Notice how each of the components has been included. The *audience* is "the fourth grade student"; the *behavior* is "to write the correct spelling"; the *condition* is "when given a list of 50 spelling words orally"; and the *degree* component is "at least 40 words." This last component represents the level of acceptable performance the teacher is willing to consider sufficient before going on. In many instances, it may not be possible for all students to get all the right answers; consequently, you should adjust your objectives accordingly.

Time to practice again. Turn to page 39.

Answers

1. when confronted with pictures of several objects—not like real life

2. in one hour when given a choice of patterns and material—not like real life—usually it takes longer to make a dress

3. for items costing more than a dollar—like real life

4. to the class without using notes—not like real life—perhaps you thought that the student would have to give speeches in other courses which you might consider real life—OK!!

5. ... when given six different shapes ... or ... as a triangle, rectangle, rhombus, square, pentagon, or parallelogram ... or ... as convex or concave . . . or ... without using their books ... (Any similar description of the task which explicates what the student is to be able to do will suffice.)

If you think you understand the condition component, go immediately back to page 37.

If you feel that you need more work on this point, read the CORD Manual, page I-17, and then turn back to page 37.

Now it's your turn to practice what you have just learned about the degree omponent. Look at each of the following examples and underline the degree ortion.

. Given 40 examples of misplaced modifiers in a paragraph, the tenth grade student will be able to recognize and underline at least 90 percent of them.

. Given a quadratic equation with numerical coefficients, the ninth grade students will be able to solve the problem to the nearest tenth.

. When placed in a lab setting with appropriate materials to choose from, the twelfth grade physics student will be able to plan an experiment to determine the charge on an electron to the nearest hundredth of an electron unit.

. Given fifteen pairs of paintings, the eleventh grade pupils will be able to determine all those painted by Renoir.

. Complete the following objective by adding a degree component: "Given six types of material, the textile students will be able to identify . . . "

_____

_____

Turn to page 40 to check your answers.

Answers

1. at least 90 percent of them

2. to the nearest tenth

3. to the nearest hundredth of an electron unit

4. all those painted by Renoir

5. All six types correctly . . .
   Five out of six correctly . . .
   Any statement which tells the student how well he must perform will suffice.

How did you do? If you got them all right, GREAT!! You are now ready for the big task: writing your very own behavioral objectives. A diagram defining a well-stated objective is given below. Study it! You might consider it to be a summary of the ABCD approach.

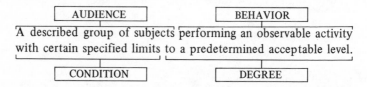

Before you launch into writing, turn first to page 42 for a comparison of the different approaches to specifying the components of behavioral objectives.

If you feel uneasy in your grasp of the four components covered in this section, please see your instructor. Then, go on to page 42.

WELCOME BACK!! You are now ready to try your hand at writing be-
avioral objectives that embody all the components you have studied as
presented by Mager or Kibler, Barker, and Miles. But first turn to page 42 for a
comparision of the three approaches to specifying the components of behavioral
objectives.

Below is an example of a behavioral objective. The components have bee
specified according to each of the three approaches. Hopefully, you will realiz
that there is no single right way to write a behavioral objective. However, ther
are several good approaches.

"When shown the appropriate letters of the alphabet, the first grade
children will be able to identify orally all of the vowels and vowel sounds."

ABCD Approach (CORD) Manual)	Kibler, Barker, and Miles Approach	Magner's Approach
Audience: "the first grade children"	*Who:* "the first grade children"	
Behavior: "to identify"	*Actual Behavior:* "to identify"	*Terminal Behavior:* "to identify"
	Results/Product: Sounds of vowels (implied orally)	
Conditions: "When shown the appropriate letters of the alphabet"	*Relevant Conditions:* "When shown the appropriate letters of of the alphabet"	*Conditions Imposed:* "When shown the appropriate letters of the alphabet"
Degree: "all of the vowels and vowel sounds"	*Standard:* "all of the vowels and vowel sounds"	*Criterion:* "all of the vowels and vowel sounds"

Now look at page 43 to try your hand at writing some well-stated behavioral
objectives.

Now that you know what the components are and have seen several examples of behavioral objectives, it is time to put your knowledge to use. The challenging task set for you is *to write three well-stated behavioral objectives without referring back to the text*. You should be prepared to identify the components of your objectives when you give them to the instructor.

Please indicate which of the approaches you are going to use in writing your behavioral objectives.

| | Mager | | Kibler et al. | | ABCD |

1. _____

_____

_____

_____

_____

2. _____

_____

_____

_____

_____

3. _____

_____

_____

_____

_____

When you have finished have your instructor check your objectives.

Why Use Behavioral Objectives?

THE TITLE OF THIS SECTION implies that there may be some doubt about the use of behavioral objectives. Does that mean you just learned how to do something that may be useless? Certainly not! But unfortunately, some educators feel that specifying behavioral objectives is too restrictive. According to their thinking, students and teachers must be free to do their own thing and to drift as the gentle intellectual breezes move them. All too often, however, when they are free and undirected, they are blown about like feathers in a hurricane. Aside from those who consider behavioral objectives restrictive, there are teachers who feel that the objectives are too much work and that they are getting paid to teach, not to write behavioral objectives. You may have known or heard of teachers who do quite well without using behavioral objectives. So why did you bother learning how to write them?

Here are some very cogent reasons why behavioral objectives will be useful to you and to your students. The primary reason is that if you, as teacher, do not

know the goals, the directions, or the objectives, you are likely to *waste* a lot of your own time as well as the students' time. Without behavioral objectives and a planned route, you will be much like the scout leader who lost his troop in the woods. The available research evidence indicates clearly that when the teacher formulates objectives, uses them in planning, and communicates them to pupils, the students will learn much more. Isn't that what teaching is about?

Ausubel's theory (1968) of advanced organizers also lends support to the practice of informing the students where they are going. Educators espousing this view might hold that behavioral objectives provide a stable cognitive structure or framework to which the students' new learning can be anchored (or as Ausubel would say, "subsumed"). Another role these advanced organizers play is to aid the student in recalling information that he already possesses that is relevant to the new learning situation or task. Consider for a moment your activities when you use a microscope. The first thing most people do is to read the directions. These directions alert you to the important steps to be followed. Why then shouldn't you give some guidelines to your students?

Secondly, there is a strong likelihood that without specific attention to objectives much teaching degenerates to passing on information and getting the students to feed it back on tests. If you begin to think about behavioral objectives, you may become aware of an excess of memory work in your teaching.

JUST
LIKE
SCHOOL

Thirdly, the task of writing objectives seems horrendous only when you are a novice. With experience, you will become faster and more proficient. Furthermore, you might find that you will have help since objectives are written by curriculum committees in many schools. You might even be lucky enough to have a set of objectives handed down to you by a previous committee or, if you are in English, in the form of a sort of encyclopedia of objectives, such as Lazarus and Knudson (1967) wrote for teachers. In the book *Selected Objectives for the English Language Arts, Grades 7-12*, Lazarus and Knudson offer a collection of objectives on various topics from which you can select and use objectives as you wish. Those of you in other fields may find Appendix A of Kibler, Barker, and Miles (1970) helpful for suggestions. Also, an objectives exchange has been started by Dr. James Popham of the Center for the Study of Evaluation at the University of California in Los Angeles. This exchange functions much like a bank, and objectives and evaluation instruments are deposited and withdrawn like currency. If you are interested in looking into the matter further, you should direct your inquiries to:

> Instructional Objectives Exchange
> Center for the Study of Evaluation
> Graduate School of Education
> University of California
> Los Angeles, California 90024

In closing this section, it might be helpful for you to consider the teaching process as an analogy to a jigsaw puzzle. What do you think some of the pieces might be?

_____

_____

_____

Turn to page 48.

By now you've probably realized that one piece of the puzzle would be *behavioral objectives*. The other two pieces are *instructional activities* and *evaluation practices*. Don't fret if you missed the last two! Now if these pieces are put together, what shape would you expect? A circle? A-ha! Right you are!

Notice that all three pieces are needed to make the picture complete.

Now, really let your imagination take hold. Picture a student at point A. Let him walk around the circle in a clockwise direction. Notice that there is a natural sequence to the events that take place. First, your imaginary student will be confronted with the behavioral objectives—that is, what he is supposed to learn. Next, he is exposed to your teaching activities—discussions, films, teacher-talk, questioning, etc. Then, the testing situation appears under evaluation processes. Note that he is now back where he started, ready for the behavioral objectives for a new concept. Also note that the interlocking character of these pieces indicates how behavioral objectives serve as guides both to the teachers in preparing their instruction and designing tests and to the students in attending to the instruction and studying for the exams.

Having finished this section, you can relate the use and the importance of behavioral objectives to the teaching process.

Now you are ready to begin climbing the eighth, ninth, and tenth rungs of the ladder of objectives shown on page 2. Why not reread the objectives? Then, turn to page 50.

Part II

How to Write Objectives at Higher Cognitive Levels

IT HAS BEEN SUGGESTED in the preceding section that it is possible to teach in such a way that the student's essential task is to memorize and feed information back to you. However, most teachers say they want to teach students to function at higher cognitive or intellectual levels. The often used cliché that teachers mutter is that they really want to "teach kids to think." Certainly, no one will deny that this is a noble ambition. But how do you go about accomplishing it? Will you achieve this end if you demonstrate your own thinking prowess, and thus serve as a model? Or will it be reached if you get a few kids to be critical of some ideas in English or civics? This line of questioning leads to a more fundamental concern: What aspects or ways of thinking could you teach?

One approach to answering this problem began in 1948 when a group of people met at a national convention and began to discuss the problems of testing for higher level cognitive processes. Eventually, a committee emerged which addressed itself to the task of formulating a taxonomy or hierarchical scheme for conceptualizing cognitive educational objectives. The committee consisted of psychologists, educators, educational psychologists, and test and measurement specialists. The work of the committee culminated in the publication in 1956 of the *Taxonomy of Educational Objectives, Handbook I: Cognitive Domain* (Bloom, 1956). They called it *Handbook I* because they planned to develop similar taxonomies for the affective and the psychomotor domains. That is, they planned to devise a hierarchical scheme for conceptualizing objectives in the feelings-attitudes-values area (affective domain) and in the physical skills area (psychomotor domain).

The purpose of *Handbook I* is to give you a way of viewing cognitive activity, thinking, or mental processes so that you can develop objectives for teaching. *Handbook I* also offers abundant illustrations of objectives at the many different cognitive levels. Unfortunately, these illustrative objectives are frequently lacking in one or more of the components needed for a well-stated behavioral objective. Pause for a moment and recall what these components are. Did you remember them all? Good! Now it's time for you to launch into learning about the Cognitive Taxonomy.

If you were to look into the Cognitive Taxonomy, you would find that it is divided into two basic or main parts: (1) Knowledge and (2) Intellectual Abilities and Skills. See the diagram on page 52.

The knowledge portion of the hierarchical cognitive scheme relates to what might be classified as retrieval operations. That is, information is stored in your central computer (or your brain, if you're anatomically inclined); and the aspect of thinking that allows you to recall or find bit and pieces of information is termed "knowledge." You might say that knowledge sounds a lot like memory. And you're right! Here's how Bloom (1956) defines the knowledge level:

> Knowledge, as defined here, involves the recall of specifics and universals, the recall of methods and processes, or the recall of a pattern, structure, or setting. For measurement purposes, the recall situation involves little more than bringing to mind the appropriate material. Although some alteration of the material may be required, this is a relatively minor part of the task. The knowledge objectives emphasize most the psychological processes of remembering. The process of relating is also involved in that a knowledge test situation requires the organization and reorganization of a problem such that it will furnish the appropriate signals and cues for the information and knowledge the individual possesses. To use an analogy, if one thinks of the mind as a file, the problem in a knowledge test situation is that of finding in the problem or task the appropriate signals, cues, and clues which will most effectively bring out whatever knowledge is filed or stored.

Bloom's definition of the knowledge level of the taxonomy is rather comprehensive. In a sense, it is a generalized summary of several more specific aspects of remembering that Bloom et al. have identified in their taxonomy. The Cognitive Taxonomy breaks down the Knowledge (level 1.00) section according to the scheme shown in Figures 1A, 1B, and 1C which briefly describes each of the different divisions and subdivisions on the knowledge level. Under each of the nine minor subdivisions, an example of a behavioral objective has been provided for you. These examples have been modified from those given in the Cognitive Taxonomy in order to present illustrations that are well-stated behavioral objectives.

For each of the major subdivisions of the knowledge level, you will be able to try your hand at writing behavioral objectives appropriate to each major subdivision (viz. 1.10—Specifics, 1.20—Ways and Means, and 1.30—Universals and Abstractions). When you finish reading about and writing knowledge level objectives, a real challenge will be presented to you: To classify objectives written at the knowledge level.

Before you study the two remaining major subdivisions of the knowledge level, why not try your hand at writing well-stated behavioral objectives (at

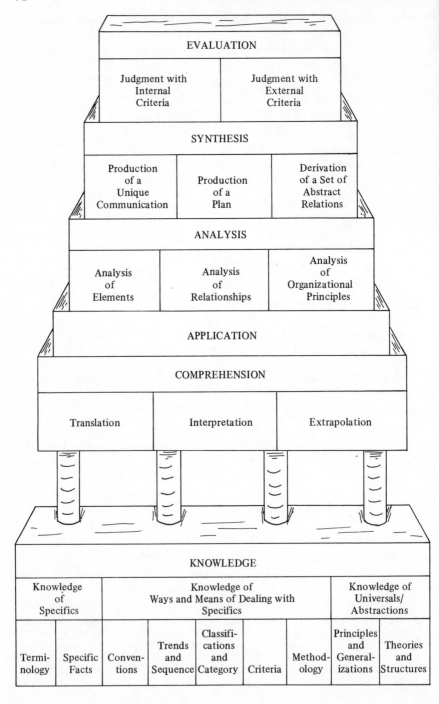

least one) that direct students to recall some *specifics*? You may choose any subject matter area you are familiar with or feel competent in for writing these objectives. A helpful guide in selecting verbs and direct objects at the various levels of the Cognitive Taxonomy has been prepared by Metfessel, Michael, and Kirsner (1969). Their scheme might prove beneficial to you in selecting verbs and direct objects that are appropriate for Knowledge of Specifics. You will find these verbs and direct objects on the fold-out front cover. The following example shows how the Metfessel et al. scheme can make your task easier.

The beginning chemistry student will be able to recall at least five elements in the atomic table having a valence of +3.

Knowledge (level 1.00)

Knowledge of Specifics (level 1.10)

The recall of specific and isolable bits of information. The emphasis is on symbols with concrete referents. This material, which is at a very low level of abstraction, may be thought of as the elements from which more complex and abstract forms of knowledge are built.

Subdivisions under level 1.10:

Knowledge of Terminology (level 1.11)

Knowledge of the referents for specific symbols (verbal and nonverbal). This may include knowledge of the most generally accepted symbol referent, knowledge of the variety of symbols which may be used for a single referent, or knowledge of the referent most appropriate to a given use of a symbol.

Given a list of technical terms in science, the eleventh grade science students will be able to define them exactly as given in the text.

Knowledge of Specific Facts (level 1.12)

Knowledge of dates, events, persons, places, etc. This may include very precise and specific information, such as the specific date or exact magnitude of a phenomenon. It may also include approximate time period or the general order of magnitude of a phenomenon.

Without using notes, the sixth grade students will be able to list all six major parts of a living cell.

FIGURE 1A
Taxonomy of Educational Objectives:
Cognitive Domain*

Note that the verb and direct object taken from Table I have been underlined for you.

*Figures 1A-6 are taken from *Taxonomy of Educational Objectives, Handbook I: Cognitive Domain*, B. S. Bloom, ed. Copyright © 1956 by David McKay Co., Inc. Reprinted by permission of the publisher.

Now it's your turn to write one or two behavioral objectives at the Knowledge of Specifics level.

(a) _____

_____

_____

(b) _____

_____

_____

Check yourself on the next page.

The following checklist will help you decide whether or not your behavioral objective measures up.

1. Does your objective contain all four (A,B,C,D) components of a well-stated behavioral objective?

    ☐ Yes   ☐ No

If "No," what element is missing? _____

2. Does the verb you used require the student to use only his memory?

    ☐ Yes   ☐ No

If you checked "No," you may have a higher level objective.

3. Does the direct object in your objective call for the student to remember some *specific* information?

    ☐ Yes   ☐ No

If you checked "No," you may have written an objective for another division of the knowledge level.

Now take a look at the next major divison of the Knowledge level: (1.20)—Knowledge of Ways and Means of Dealing with Specifics—beginning on page 56.

Knowledge of Ways and Means of Dealing with Specifics (1.20)

Knowledge of the ways of organizing, studying, judging, and criticizing. This includes the methods of inquiry, the chronological sequences, and the standards of judgment within a field as well as the patterns of organization through which the areas of the fields themselves are determined and internally organized. This knowledge is at an intermediate level of abstraction between specific knowledge on the one hand and knowledge of universals on the other. It does not so much demand the activity of the student in using the materials as it does a more passive awareness of their nature.

Subdivisions under level 1.20:

Knowledge of Conventions (level 1.21)

Knowledge of characteristic ways of treating and presenting ideas and phenomena. For purposes of communication and consistency, workers in a field employ usages, styles, practices, and forms which best suit their purposes and/or which appear to suit best the phenomena with which they deal. It should be recognized that although these forms and conventions are likely to be set up on arbitrary, accidental, or authoritative bases, they are retained because of the general agreement or concurrence of individuals concerned with the subject, phenomena, or problem.

When given several samples of poetry, the tenth grade English students will be able to identify the forms correctly in all cases.

Knowledge of Trends and Sequences (level 1.22)

Knowledge of the processes, directions, and movement of phenomena with respect to time.

When given a series of historical events, the eighth grade history student will be able to order them chronologically with no mistakes.

Knowledge of Classifications and Categories (level 1.23)

Knowledge of the classes, sets, divisions, and arrangements which are regarded as fundamental for a given subject field, purpose, argument, or problem.

When given a particular genus, the tenth grade biology student will be able to recall all the subdivisons.

Knowledge of Criteria (level 1.24)

Knowledge of the criteria by which facts, principles, opinions, and conduct are tested or judged.

FIGURE 1B
Taxonomy of Educational Objectives:
Cognitive Domain

When given a sonnet, the eleventh grade English student will be able to recall and name all of the criteria necessary for a good sonnet.

Knowledge of Methodology (level 1.25)

Knowledge of the methods of inquiry, techniques, and procedures employed in a particular subject field as well as those employed in investigating particular problems and phenomena. The emphasis here is on the individual's knowledge of the method rather than on his ability to use the method.

Given a sample of metal, the industrial arts student will be able to identify the techniques for annealing metal.

FIGURE 1B (continued)
Taxonomy of Educational Objectives:
Cognitive Domain

It may help to pause at this juncture in order to practice writing objectives that require students to demonstrate knowledge of ways and means of dealing with specifics. As before, you may select any content areas or subject matter you are knowledgeable in to write your behavioral objectives. The following example with the Metfessel, Michael, and Kirsner infinitives and direct object underlined might help you get started.

When given a specific type of burn, the first aid students will be able to identify correctly from a list of five possible treatments the proper treatment to give the burn.

You'll find other suggested infinitives and direct objects on the fold-out front cover.

Try to write two objectives within this *major* subdivision (1.20) of the Knowledge level.

(a) _____

_____

_____

(b) _____

_____

_____

Check yourself on page 58.

Evaluate your objectives in terms of the following criteria:

a. Are all the components of a behavioral objective contained in those you wrote?

	Yes		No

If "No," what component was missing? _____

---

b. Are students required to merely *remember* something in order to fulfill your objective?

	Yes		No

If not, you probably have a higher level objective, since you are requiring students to do more than recall or retrieve stored information.

c. Do your objectives require students to recognize *conventions*, *trends*, *categories*, *criteria*, or *methods*?

	Yes		No

This exercise was probably quite easy for you because teachers frequently ask these types of questions on exams. But note that even though students are required to know (i.e., remember, recall, or recognize) uses for specifics, it remains only a memory function.

To complete the Knowledge level of Bloom's Cognitive Taxonomy look at page 59 for the third major subdivision: 1.30 Knowledge of Universals and Abstractions.

In completing the last section of the Knowledge level, you should be able to write a Knowledge level behavioral objective that requires your students to remember some universals or abstractions. Again, you will find helpful guides in selecting infintives and direct objects appropriate for objectives at the 1.31 and 1.32 levels. See the front cover fold-out. Here's an example that you might consider.

Without using notes or texts, the twelfth grade physics student will be able to recall the three laws of thermodynamics exactly as stated.

Knowledge of the Universals and Abstractions in a Field (level 1.30)

Knowledge of the major schemes and patterns by which phenomena and ideas are organized. These are the large structures, theories, and generalizations which dominate a subject field or which are quite generally used in studying phenomena or solving problems. These are at the highest levels of abstraction and complexity.

Subdivisions under level 1.30:

Knowledge of Principles and Generalizations (level 1.31)

Knowledge of particular abstractions which summarize observations of phenomena. These are the abstractions which are of value in explaining, describing, predicting or in determining the most appropriate and relevant action or direction to be taken.

When given a geometric proof, the tenth grade geometry student will be able to recognize and state the principle involved.

Knowledge of Theories and Structures (level 1.32)

Knowledge of the *body* of principles and generalizations together with their interrelations which present a clear, rounded, and systematic view of a complex phenomenon, problem, or field. These are the most abstract formulations, and they can be used to show the interrelations and organization of a great range of specifics.

When given a short passage expounding a particular form of government, the twelfth grade civics students will be able to identify orally from which theory of government the passage would be taken.

FIGURE 1C
Taxonomy of Educational Objectives:
Cognitive Domain

For your subject area or area of special interest, write a behavioral objective at the Knowledge of Universals and Abstractions level of the taxonomy. Identify which of the two sub-categories your objective belongs.

_____

_____

_____

_____

[   ] Level 1.31   [   ] Level 1.32

Turn to page 63 to evaluate your objective.

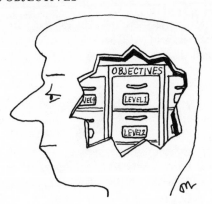

Now that you have become acquainted with the subdivisions of the Knowledge level of the taxonomy, you will have a chance to try classifying some objectives according to the various levels. A series of nine Knowledge level objectives has been stated below. The first one has been classified for you as level 1.12, Knowledge of Specific Facts. Your task is to classify the remaining eight objectives according to the appropriate level in the Knowledge section of the taxonomy. You may have to refer back to the text for some of the finer distinctions. Good Luck!

1. The eighth grade history student will be able to give the exact dates for seven major Civil War battles when the names of the battles are given to him.

   Classification: 1.12, Knowledge of Specific Facts

2. Given a list of ten vocabulary words, the sixth grade student will be able to correctly define in writing at least eight of them.

   Classification:

3. The twelfth grade physics student will be able to recall and write all the appropriate laws covering a gravity experiment that has been demonstrated in the lab.

   Classification:

4. When given a group of spelling words, the fourth grade student will be able to state orally the rules that he uses to spell each word.

   Classification:

5. After viewing a short film clip, the education student will be able to recognize and state all the methods the teacher in the film was using in her instruction.

   Classification:

6. When shown a monthly series of graphs depicting changes in the economy, the senior economics student will be able to identify all the influences affecting price changes.

   Classification: _____

7. Given a series of developmental events in history, the tenth grade student will be able to identify in writing the correct theory which subsumes these events.

   Classification: _____

8. When shown slides of the various types of furniture, the eleventh grade home economics student will be able to identify the appropriate category in all cases.

   Classification: _____

9. After having written a descriptive essay, the ninth grade English student will be able to name orally five standards for judging the quality of descriptive essays.

   Classification: _____

Now turn to page 64 to check your classifications against those intended.

Check your objective for the following points.

. Does it contain all the components of a well-stated behavioral objective?

| | Yes | | No |

If "No," which element is missing? _____

. Does your objective require the students to function only in recall or memory capacity?

| | Yes | | No |

If you checked "No," you may have written a higher level objective.

. Is the direct object in your behavioral objective some universal or generalization?

| | Yes | | No |

If not, you probably wrote a lower level of objective.

After reaching this point, if you have any questions regarding Knowledge level objectives, why not check with your instructor? If you feel confident that you have mastered this section of the taxonomy, TERRIFIC!!! Turn back to pages 61 and 62 for a real challenge.

Intended Classifications

1. 1.12

2. 1.11

3. 1.31

4. 1.21

5. 1.25

6. 1.22

7. 1.32

8. 1.23

9. 1.24

If you missed more than three, you should go back to page 53 and reread the material on the Knowledge levels. If you still have trouble distinguishing the levels, consult your instructor.

If you got six or more right, give yourself a pat on the back. You're doing GREAT!!! After rewarding yourself go to page 65.

The second section of the Cognitive Taxonomy deals with "Intellectual Abilities and Skills," which you can think of in terms of processing operations as opposed to simple retrieval operations on the Knowledge level. That is, the information either stored in or provided to your central computer is processed or modified in some way. The aspects of thinking that define these processes are referred to as comprehension, application, analysis, synthesis, and evaluation. Now you say, "That sounds like thinking!" Well, you're right in a sense. But memory plays an integral part even at these higher levels. You must remember or know some specific information before you can hope to analyze it. Recall the diagram on page 52, and note how the higher levels of cognitive functioning are supported by pillars resting on a foundation of "knowledge." Bloom et al. have emphasized these functional relationships among the various levels by including the word "taxonomy" in the title of their book. A taxonomy implies a hierarchical structure, i.e. a sort of staircase if you like. For a more formal definition of this section, Bloom (1956) defines Intellectual Abilities and Skills as follows:

Abilities and skills refer to organized modes of operation and generalized techniques for dealing with materials and problems. The materials and problems may be of such a nature that little or no specialized and technical information is required. Such information as is required can be assumed to be part of the individual's general fund of knowledge. Other problems may require specialized and technical information at a rather high level such that specific knowledge and skill in dealing with the problem and the materials are required. The ability and skill objectives emphasize the mental processes of organizing and reorganizing material to achieve a particular purpose. The materials may be given or remembered.

As indicated previously, this definition contains many levels. In fact, the Cognitive Taxonomy breaks down intellectual skills and abilities into five major levels. Under each of these major levels as shown in Figures 2,3,4,5, and 6, several subdivisions have been made. For each subdivision you are given a brief explanation, as well as an illustrative behavioral objective. After you study each of the five *major* levels in the second part of the Cognitive Taxonomy, you will have the opportunity to write behavioral objectives corresponding to the various levels. Before you launch into the comprehension level, you may find it helpful to turn back to page 2 and review rungs 8, 9, and 10 of the behavioral objective ladder for this unit.

Comprehension (level 2.00)

This represents the lowest level of understanding. It refers to a type of understanding or apprehension such that the individual knows what is being communicated and can make use of the material or idea being communicated without necessarily relating it to other material or seeing its fullest implications.

Subdivisions under level 2.00:

Translation (level 2.10)

Comprehension as evidenced by the care and accuracy with which the communication is paraphrased or rendered from one language or form of communication to another. Translation is judged on the basis of faithfulness and accuracy, that is, on the extent to which the material in the original communication is preserved even though the form of the communication has been altered.

Given ten sentences in French and without the use of outside resources, the first year French student will be able to translate correctly into English at least seven out of ten sentences.

(Notice how the objective at this level implies the lower level, that is, knowledge of French vocabulary words.)

Interpretation (level 2.20)

The explanation or summarization of a communication. Whereas translation involves an objective part-for-part rendering of a communication, interpretation involves a reordering, rearrangement, or a new view of the material.

The eleventh grade English student when given a poem for the first time will be able to state in his own words the main idea of each verse.

Extrapolation (level 2.30)

The extension of trends or tendencies beyond the given data to determine implications, consequences, corollaries, effects, etc., which are in accordance with the condition described in the original communication.

Given a graph showing steel production for the last five years, the economics student will be able to predict within five percent the steel production in tons five years hence.

FIGURE 2
Taxonomy of Educational Objectives:
Cognitive Domain

Before going on to the next level, why not attempt writing some behavioral objectives which involve translation, interpretation, *or* extrapolation? As in previous exercises, you might find Metfessel's et al. infinitives and direct objects useful aids in writing your own objectives for whatever subject matter you feel competent to write on. Using these aids (which you'll find inside the front fold-out), the following sample objective was developed.

Given a hypothetical experiment, the physics students will be able <u>to differentiate</u> between the wave and particle <u>theories</u> of light.

Note the underlined infinitive and direct object taken from Metfessel, Michael, and Kirsner for the interpretation level.

Now it's your turn to write a Comprehension level behavioral objective. (One objective will suffice.)

_____

_____

_____

_____

Check your objective with the criteria on the next page.

Here are two criteria your objective should measure up to.

a. Contains all components of a well-stated behavioral objective.

b. The verb should imply one of the three subdivisions under comprehension: translation, interpretation, or extrapolation. Preferably, you did not use the verb "to understand"—a trap which many beginning objective writers fall into.

Note that the behavior expected of the students should denote his performance of some form of cognitive processing beyond the memory level.

If your Comprehension level objective satisfies these meager criteria "Congratulations!!" You've got the hang of it. Turn to page 69.

Perhaps you're still having some trouble sorting out the differences between the various levels. Why not check with your instructor or, if you prefer, read Bloom's et al. detailed description of the Comprehension level on pages 89-96 in *Taxonomy of Educational Objectives* (Bloom, 1956). When you think you've caught on, begin reading about Application level objectives on the next page.

Application (level 3.00)

The use of abstractions in particular and concrete situations. The abstractions may be in the form of general ideas, rules of procedures, or generalized methods. The abstractions may also be technical principles, ideas, and theories which must be remembered and applied.

When given five examples of change in dimensions but with constant volume, the fourth grade student will be able to apply the principles of conservation correctly in each case.

FIGURE 3
Taxonomy of Educational Objectives:
Cognitive Domain

That was a short section! You may want to reread it carefully before trying o write an Application level objective. On the back fold-out, you'll find a ontinuation of the Metfessel, Michael, and Kirsner guide for some of the ppropriate infinitives and direct objects. The following example illustrates one /pe of objective that you could write in this exercise.

Given problems containing two unknowns, the eighth grade student will be able <u>to choose</u> two correct <u>procedures</u> for solving word problems in algebra.

Try writing an Application level behavioral objective for your subject matter a the space below.

_____

_____

_____

_____

_____

When you're finished turn to page 70.

Well, that was probably an easy objective for you to write. One cautionary note is in order, however. The task set for the student should be at least slightly different from the teacher's instruction. Otherwise, the student who merely can remember what the teacher did will be able to fulfil the objective although he might not be able to apply or use his knowledge of the principles, laws, theories etc., in similar but unfamiliar situations.

Again, check your objective for the components of a well-stated behavioral objective.

Then, determine for yourself (or ask a fellow student in the same subject matter area) if your objective requires the student to use his knowledge in different situations or circumstances.

If you are unsure, you could consult Bloom et al. for a detailed explanation or you could check with your instructor.

Look at the next page for the next level in the Cognitive Taxonomy.

Analysis (level 4.00)

The breakdown of a communication into its constituent elements or parts such that the relative hierarchy of ideas is made clear and/or the relations between the ideas expressed are made explicit. Such analyses are intended to clarify the communication, to indicate how the communication is organized, and to detail the way in which it manages to convey its effects, as well as its basis and arrangement.

Subdivisions under level 4.00:

Analysis of Elements (level 4.10)

Identification of the elements included in a communication.

Given a mathematical proof, the geometry student will be able to distinguish all of the underlying assumptions.

Analysis of Relationships (level 4.20)

The connections and interactions between elements and parts of a communication.

When given an unfamiliar painting to be analyzed, the art student will be able to analyze the interrelationships of color and form.

Analysis of Organizational Principles (level 4.30)

The organization, systematic arrangement, and structure which hold the communication together. This includes the "explicit" as well as the "implicit" structure. It includes the bases, necessary arrangement, and mechanics which made the communication a unit.

When confronted with a political debate on tape, the senior debate students will be able to analyze the structural viewpoint of all the arguments presented.

FIGURE 4
Taxonomy of Educational Objectives:
Cognitive Domain

Time to put into practice what you've learned about the Analysis level. In his exercise you should develop at least one objective requiring the student to function analytically—that is, the student is directed to break down into its constituent parts or to show relationships between component parts or to deduce the organizational structure of the material. Some verbs and direct objects are listed on the back fold out which may be helpful to you in writing your behavioral objective. Perhaps another example will help you get started.

When given samples of finished garments the tenth grade girls in home economics will be able to distinguish between all the particulars of various types of hems.

For your subject area, write one or two Analysis level behavioral objectives below.

(a) _____

_____

_____

_____

(b) _____

_____

_____

_____

Finished? GREAT!! Charge on to the Synthesis level on the next page.

Synthesis (level 5.00)

The putting together of elements and parts so as to form a whole. This involves the process of working with pieces, parts, elements, etc., and arranging and combining them in such a way as to constitute a pattern or structure not clearly there before.

Subdivisions under level 5.00:

Production of a Unique Communication (level 5.10)

The development of a communication in which the writer or speaker attempts to convey ideas, feelings, and/or experiences to others.

The eleventh grade science student, having finished a unit on sources of power and given sufficient time outside of class, will be able to write a minimum 500-word essay that expounds his ideas on the uses of solar radiation.

Production of a Plan or Proposed Set of Operations (5.20)

The development of a plan of work or the proposal of a plan of operations. The plan should satisfy requirements of the task which may be given to the student or which he may develop for himself.

Using their own body measurements, the twelfth grade home economics girls will be able to design a well-fitting dress pattern.

Derivation of a Set of Abstract Relations (level 5.30)

The development of a set of abstract relations either to classify or to explain particular data or phenomena; or the deduction of propositions and relations from a set of basic propositions or symbolic representations.

Given a set of empirical data, the senior math students will be able to derive a mathematical equation that fits the data.

FIGURE 5
Taxonomy of Educational Objectives:
Cognitive Domain

Before you finish up the second part of the taxonomy, you should practice writing objectives in your area at level five—synthesis. Your efforts here will focus on directing students to draw things, ideas, parts, or whatnots into a unified whole. This level represents the counterpart to analysis (breaking apart) inasmuch as synthesis objectives require students to complete or to put something together. Creative endeavors typically fall in this level of the taxonomy where the individual produces, plans or derives responses that are uniquely personal. Help in phrasing objectives at this level is available from Metfessel's et al. guide to verbs and direct objects. You'll find the Synthesis level on the back fold-out.

Produce one well-stated behavioral objective for your subject matter specialty.

_____

_____

_____

_____

_____

_____

See some check points on page 76.

Evaluation (level 6.00)

Judgments about the value of material and methods for given purposes. Quantitative and qualitative judgments about the extent to which material and methods satisfy criteria. Use of a standard of appraisal. The criteria may be those determined by the student or those which are given to him.

Subdivisions under level 6.00:

Judgments in Terms of Internal Evidence (level 6.10)

Evaluation of the accuracy of a communication from such evidence as logical accuracy, consistency, and other internal criteria.

When given a statement of experimental results, the students in physics will be able to assess all the scientific fallacies in the report.

Judgments in Terms of External Criteria (level 6.20)

Evaluation of material with reference to selected or remembered criteria.

When given a sample essay to judge, the twelfth grade English students will be able to judge an essay in terms of the criteria for a good descriptive essay.

FIGURE 6
Taxonomy of Educational Objectives:
Cognitive Domain

Your last writing task in this section is to develop one behavioral objective at the evaluation level. Key words are again provided on the back fold-out. Here's one last example for you to consider.

The senior art student will be able to contrast the works of Picasso and Van Gogh in terms of the standards developed in this course.

Now, write one objective that requires your students (present or future) to function on the evaluation level. You may write one in terms of either internal or external criteria.

When you're through writing this objective, turn to page 77.

CHECK

B. H. Objectives		5097
125 School Drive		
College, U.S.A.	_____ 19 ___	$\frac{75\text{-}1667\text{-}}{910}$
Pay to the		
Order of _____	$ _____	
_____ Dollars		
First College Bank	_____	

POINT

Did you include all the components of a well-stated behavioral objective? (Do you remember what they are?)

Does your objective require individuals specified in the audience component to behave in a manner which denotes their ability to formulate a unique plan or production of some sort?

If you are still confused or in doubt regarding what synthesis means, read pages 162-176 in Bloom's *Taxonomy of Educational Objectives*.

Then, take three deep breaths! And rally your energies and hang on for one more level: Evaluation.

Turn back to page 75.

Why are you studying the levels of the Cognitive Taxonomy? Isn't this supposed to be a unit on behavioral objectives? What's the connection? Well, you will recall that this discussion of the Cognitive Taxonomy began with the implied condition that you as teachers (prospective or present) want your students to think. But in order to reach this goal, you need a plan of some sort. Well, the Cognitive Taxonomy fits the bill quite well. It represents a scheme developed by scholars to help you consider the kinds of thinking or cognitive functions which an individual can learn or learn to do better. In a sense, Bloom's hierarchical structure is a path you can follow as you lead your students to the higher levels of thought.

Now turn to page 78 for some practice classifiying objectives at the higher levels. Feel free to look back as needed. You could jot down brief descriptions of what each level means to you. A short summary of this sort will help you zero in on the right level.

K _____

_____

C _____

_____

A _____

_____

A _____

_____

S _____

_____

E _____

_____

How well can you classify behavioral objectives according to Bloom's taxonomy? Here's your chance to climb the ninth rung of the objective ladder for this unit. You will be given several objectives and asked to classify them according to the major and minor levels in the Cognitive Taxonomy. Note that some objectives may contain two or more levels. Here's an example to get you started.

The student majoring in art will be able to examine a work of art and identify the major line and color components and the relationships among them.

Classification: 4.10 and 4.20 (Analysis)

This objective would be classified as a combination of levels 4.10, Analysis of Elements, and level 4.20, Analysis of Relationships, under the major level Analysis.

Now try your hand at classifying the following objectives.

1. Using the five principles for organizing units, the student teacher will be able to plan a unit of instruction in his subject matter area.

   Classification: _____

2. When given a sample report he has not seen before, the chemistry student will be able to translate correctly a technical lab report into layman's language.

   Classification: _____

3. The physics student enrolled in thermodynamics will be able to apply the first law of thermodynamics in solving a problem of heat transfer within a tolerance of five percent.

   Classification: _____

4. Given the standards for a gear design, the pupils in industrial arts will be able to judge whether to accept or to reject a sample gear in terms of those standards.

   Classification: _____

5. The beginning music student will be able to name all of the criteria which were discussed in class for evaluating a musical composition. (Be careful!)

   Classification: _____

6. When given an unfamiliar poem, the students in English 105 will be able to identify 80 percent of the alliterative elements of the poem.

   Classification: _____

7. When given a graph of commodity prices for 1960-1970, the economics student will be able to determine within two cents the average price of milk in 1965.

   Classification: _____

8. When given a bridge network, a physics student will be able to use Ohm's Law to solve for the impedance to the nearest tenth of an ohm.

   Classification: _____

   Turn to page 80 for the intended classifications.

Intended Classifications

1. (Synthesis) 5.20, Production of a Plan or Proposed Set of Operations.

2. (Comprehension) 2.10, Translation

3. (Application) 3.00, Application

4. (Evaluation) 6.20, Judgments in Terms of External Criteria

5. (Knowledge) 1.24, Knowledge of Criteria

6. (Analysis) 4.10, Analysis of Elements

7. (Comprehension) 2.30, Extrapolation

8. (Application) 3.00, Application

How did you do? If you got all the major levels correct, you have mastered the basics down. If you got most of the minor levels correct, you are very astute. Some minor level classifications and even some major level ones are subject to interpretation; and two people will not always agree on the classifications for the same objective. This may have happened to you in this exercise. But if you can justify the reasoning behind your choice of a particular level, you are analyzing the situation—an important first step.

If you missed most of the intended classifications on the major levels, you had better consult your instructor. You may need help!!!

Now you are ready for the last rung on the ladder of objectives and for something really challenging. Turn to page 82 and Part III. But take a break before you do. You deserve it!

Part III

How to Make a Specification Chart for Behavioral Objectives

HAVING REACHED THIS POINT in the unit, you should be well-aware that there are two major problems in the task of writing objectives. First, there is the problem of analyzing and organizing your subject matter. And second, there is the problem of writing objectives at different and appropriate levels of the Cognitive Taxonomy. How do you decide which material is important and how it should be sequenced? The answer to these questions is in your professional preparation—you must become knowledgeable about your subject area, its parts, its sequences, and its organization. In addition, you may be helped by fellow teachers and curriculum committees.

As far as the second problem is concerned, the level of your objectives depends on what you or your school system want to accomplish in educating the students. You are faced with a choice between levels on which the students will be able to function as a result of your instruction. But remember that it is not a very gratifying, stimulating, or worthwhile function if your teaching can be described as "training parrots to perform."

A helpful guide for relating content material to levels of cognitive functioning is a two-way grid called a "specification chart." On the vertical axis, the teacher or test designer lists the important ideas or major points that have been covered during the instructional process. Typically, this listing takes the form of an outline of what is presented to the students—the course content. Along the horizontal axis, the *major* levels (K-C-A-A-S-E) of the Cognitive Taxonomy are specified.(See the chart on the next page.)

Originally, this grid was used for developing test questions relative to particular items in the subject matter outline at various levels of the taxonomy. Another way of looking at it is to consider the specification chart a "blueprint" (a design developed by an architect which serves as a guide for building a finished structure). How well the blueprint is laid out and how well it is followed determine in great measure what the final structure will be like. The blueprint and construction correspond to the teacher's plan and presentation of in-

◄────── Horizontal Axis ──────► Major Levels of Cognitive Taxonomy

Content Outline	Knowledge	Comprehension	Application	Analysis	Synthesis	Evaluation
I. ᴜᴜᴜᴜ						
A. ᴜᴜᴜᴜ						
B. ᴜᴜᴜᴜ						
C. ᴜᴜᴜᴜ						
II. ᴜᴜᴜᴜ						
A. ᴜᴜᴜ						
B. ᴜᴜᴜᴜ						

struction. Recall the three-part puzzle on page 48, which interrelated behavioral objectives, instructional activity, and evaluation.

As an illustration of how a specification chart is developed, consider a biology teacher who is teaching a unit on the "Classification of Isolating Mechanisms" as part of a series on evolution. After considering the proper sequencing of the content, the teacher might arrange the subject matter according to the following outline.

Classification of Isolating Mechanisms

I. Pre-mating Mechanisms
   A. Seasonal and Habitat Isolation
   B. Ethological Isolation
   C. Mechanical Isolation
II. Post-mating Mechanisms
   A. Gametic Mortality
   B. Zygotic Mortality
   C. Hybrid Inviability
   D. Hybrid Sterility

This outline is simply used as the left-hand vertical axis as illustrated in the specification chart on page 84.

Having decided what to teach and having arranged the content on the vertical axis of the two-way grid, the teacher writes the levels of the Cognitive Taxonomy on the horizontal axis. After the biology teacher has the top margins of the specification chart filled in, he is left with a lot of empty boxes or spaces. What do you think he does now? Right! He writes behavioral objectives. But note that he knows exactly what material or content he is going to teach and test and, in addition, knows precisely what level he expects the students to perform at. For example, one objective for item I-B of the content outline, "Ethological Isolation," is at the comprehension level; that is, the teacher expects the students not only to memorize what ethological isolation is but to translate

SPECIFICATION CHART FOR UNIT ON CLASSIFICATION OF ISOLATING MECHANISMS

Content Outline	Knowledge	Comprehension	Application	Analysis	Synthesis	Evaluation
I. Pre-mating Mechanisms	The biology students will be able to name the three types of isolation.		When given a sample population of fruit flies, the students will be able to choose the correct process(es) that led to isolation.			
A. Seasonal and Habitat Isolation				When given a series of slides depicting environmental conditions, the biology students will be able to discriminate between the types of isolation. (This objective applies to all parts of section I in the outline.)		Given the effectiveness and amount of insecticide used, the biology students will be able to judge the effects of DDT on mating.
B. Ethological Isolation		Citing an appropriate example, the biology students will be able to define in their own words the meaning of ethological isolation.				
C. Mechanical Isolation	The biology students will be able to list from memory the six forms of mechanical isolation.					
II. Post-mating Mechanisms	The biology students will be able to name the four post-mating mechanisms.			The biology students will be able to analyze a given population to determine which mechanism(s) affected the demise of the species. (This objective applies to all subheadings under section II of the outline for this unit.)		When given specific determinants for the post-mating mechanisms, the biology students will be able to judge in terms of the theory of evolution the resultant condition of a particular species. (This objective applies to all subheadings under section II of this outline.)
A. Gametic Mortality			When given a sample of ants to control, the students will be able to apply the laws for gametic mortality.			
B. Zygotic Mortality		The biology students will be able to infer the effects of zygotic mortality on evolution.				
C. Hybrid Inviability					The biology students will be able to develop an hypothesis regarding the effects of partial hybrid inviability.	
D. Hybrid Sterility		The biology students will be able to draw conclusions given partial hybrid sterility.				

book words into their own. Note that some objectives, especially those at higher levels of the taxonomy, can encompass several items in the content outline. The teacher decides what level as well as what content is appropriate in writing the objectives. Examine the chart on the preceding page.

Now that you have studied the sample specification chart for "Isolating Mechanisms," you may wonder why some boxes were filled in and others left blank. Recall that the teacher decides at what level he wants the students to be able to perform. Thus, he has options for choosing at which levels he will teach various aspects of the content outline. Moreover, objectives at certain levels of the taxonomy may not always be meaningful or teachable. Notice that the teacher in the example is clearly cognizant of those levels he has chosen to teach at as well as at which levels the students will be able to perform.

Are there any other advantages to a specification chart besides indicating to the teacher which levels the teaching is being directed toward? Certainly there are! Consider the architect and his blueprints again. How do the subcontractors know what to do? Right! They follow the blueprint. Students are also guided by your behavioral objectives in studying the content material. But how does the architect know the structure he designed was properly built? Inspectors check the building against the specifications in the blueprint. By analogy, the teacher tests the students on the objective he has specified. And, just as it would be unfair to inspect a warehouse for nonspecified chandeliers, it is unfair for teachers to evaluate students on subject matter or levels of cognitive functioning that were not specified in the blueprint of objectives.

With a blueprint as a guide, the architect can show other architects and city planners what he plans to build, and he can share his ideas via the concrete medium of a blueprint. This same course of action is open to you as teachers through the use of specification charts as an aid to communication in dealing with parents, administrators, and school boards.

Here's another example of a specification chart. This one was developed for a unit on "Research Articles." The content outline specified for the course is shown below.

    I. Research Methodologies
       A. Case Studies
       B. Surveys
       C. Experiments
   II. Research Designs
       A. True Experiment
       B. Quasi-experiment
 III. Statistical Tools
       A. Sources
       B. Types
       C. Application

IV. Research Articles
  A. Introduction
  B. Review of Literature
  C. Procedures
  D. Results
  E. Discussion

Look carefully at the chart on the next page.

Note that some higher level objectives may include several entries in the subject matter outline. In some instances, the nature of the subject will dictate the grouping of items in the outline in order to achieve a meaningful objective. In any event, the specification chart shows the teacher at what level he is asking students to perform. It further serves as a guide to the student in the learning encounter via the behavioral objectives and to the teacher in the process of evaluation.

In closing this section, you will be required to demonstrate your mastery by developing a *small* specification chart of the type shown on pages 84 and 87. are the steps to follow in developing your blueprint.

1. Pick a *brief* topic (keep it small and manageable.)

2. Break the topic down into its constituent parts and organize them sequentially as you would when teaching.

If you are in doubt as to how to proceed in steps 1 and 2, you might find the examples in Figure 7 on page 88 helpful. Observe that most outlines are quite simple, and try to keep yours that way. Using a complicated outline for your attempt at a specification chart will probably only compound your difficulties.

3. Arrange your content outline from step 2 down the left side of the page and the major levels of the Cognitive Taxonomy across the top as illustrated in example specification charts

4. In the pigeonholes created by crossing your outline with the taxonomy, begin to write objectives in those boxes which you feel should be filled in light of the content material you have chosen.

SPECIFICATION CHART FOR UNIT ON RESEARCH ARTICLES

Outline	Knowledge	Comprehension	Application	Analysis	Synthesis	Evaluation
I. Research Methodologies A. Case Studies B. Surveys C. Experiments	The students will be able to recall the various methodologies on a short answer completion test. (1.11)	Given hypothetical research questions; the students will be able to state them in the null hypothesis format. (2.10)				
II. Research Designs A. True Experiment B. Quasi-Experiment	On a multiple choice test, the students will be able to recognize in all cases the best definition of various terms commonly used in research. (1.11)	Given a statement of a fictional research design, the students will be able to write out the appropriate symbolic notation. (2.10)	The students will be able to apply Campbell and Stanley's guidelines for threats to internal validity to a specific hypothetical research design. The students will list weaknesses and appropriate remedies. (3.00)	Provided with a novel research design, the students will be able to analyze the design in terms of the elements of the pea-picker model. (4.10)	When exposed for the first time to a specific problem, the students will be able to devise an appropriate research design to test the alternative hypotheses. (5.20)	Provided with a research article and sufficient time (one week), the students will be able to evaluate the publishability of the article in terms of the criteria requisite for good research. The students must provide reasons to justify their recommendations. (6.20) (This objective covers items I through IV in the outline.)
III. Statistical Tools A. Sources B. Types C. Applications	The students will be able to list at least five resource persons to whom they might go for guidance and/or assistance. (1.12)	Provided with graphs showing interactions, the students will be able to specify in writing all the implications in terms of the coordinate labels. (2.20)	Using a selection of raw data from a fictional research problem, the students will be able to apply the appropriate statistical procedures in order to test the hypothesis. (3.00)			
IV. Research Articles A. Introduction B. Review of Literature C. Procedures D. Results E. Discussion		The students will be able to state in their own words the logic underlying the format for a typical research article. (2.20)		Given results and the author's conclusions, the students will be able to determine if the author is consistent in the report. (4.20) From an abstract of an article, the students will be able to distinguish the major components. (4.10)	The students will be able to make a presentation to the class that shows the interrelationship between a selected sample of five research articles from their field of study. (5.10)	Supplied with a procedures section and a table of results from a research article, the students will be able to decide if the results are consistent and if not, to specify the inconsistencies. In either case, the students must state reasons. (6.10)

Artistic Composition

I. Elements of Design
II. Principles of Design
III. Lettering
IV. Use of Different Media

The Human Eye

I. Eye Structure
   A. Location
   B. Function
II. Eye Problems
   A. Refraction
   B. Color Vision Deficiency
   C. Night Blindness
III. Eye Care

Life on Earth

I. Origin of Life on Earth
   A. Early Life Forms
   B. Proconsul Apes
II. Pleistocene Hominids
   A. Homo Sapiens
   B. Homo Erectus

Effects of Civil War on the South

I. Why South Went to War
II. Why South Was Unable to Win
III. Cost in Manpower to South
IV. Economic Effects of the Civil War

Ideal Gas Law (PU = nRT)

I. Definition of Gas
II. Effects of Pressure (P)
III. Effects of Volume (V)
IV. Effects of Temperature (T)
V. Effects of "n"

Wildlife Conservation and Extinction

I. Methods of Extinction
   A. Direct Assault
   B. Indirect Reduction
II. Characteristics of the Extinction-Prone
   A. Food Preferences
   B. Breeding Habits
   C. Restrictive Range

FIGURE 7
Sample Content Outlines

You should try to have at least one objective for each major level of the taxonomy. Perhaps you may be able to use some of the other objectives you have written in this unit. You may use the form for a specification chart provided on pages 90 and 91, or you may develop one on your own. When you finish, take your specification chart to your instructor for discussion.

After your chart has been reviewed, turn to page 93. GOOD LUCK!!

CONTENT OUTLINE		

Summary

You have just finished a comprehensive self-instructional unit on defining and writing behavioral objectives at various levels of cognitive functioning. It is hoped that you will remember the basic aspects of a behavioral objective. But more important, you have learned a planned approach for developing what you are going to teach, for clarifying to students what it is they are expected to learn (to do), for evaluating the outcomes of your instruction, and for communicating to others what you have tried to accomplish. Simple tools such as behavioral objectives can surely help you do a better job of teaching. Why not be a SUPER-TEACHER, USE BEHAVIORAL OBJECTIVES!!!

You may want to review briefly the objectives outlined for you on page 2. This review process will alert you to the specific skills and competencies that you should have acquired as a result of working through this text.

References

Ausubel, D. P. *Educational psychology: A cognitive view.* New York: Holt, Rinehart and Winston, Inc., 1968.

Bloom, B. S. (Ed.) *Taxonomy of educational objectives. Handbook I: Cognitive domain.* New York: David McKay Co., 1956.

Kibler, R. J., Barker, L. L., & Miles, D. T. *Behavioral objectives and instruction.* Boston: Allyn and Bacon, Inc., 1970.

Lazarus, A. L., & Knudson, R. *Selected objectives for the English language arts, grades 7-12.* Boston: Houghton Mifflin Co., 1967.

Mager, R. F *Preparing instructional objectives.* Palo Alto, California: Fearon Publishers, Inc., 1962.

Metfessel, N. S., Michael, W. B., & Kirsner, D. A. Instrumentation of Bloom's and Krathwohl's taxonomies for the writing of educational objectives. *Psychology in the schools,* 1969, (3), 227-231.

Paulson, C. F. and Nelson, F. G. Behavioral objectives, in Crawford, Jack, (ed.) *CORD national research training manual.* Oregon State System of Higher Education (Teaching Research Division), 1969.

Payne, D. A. *The specification and measurement of learning outcomes.* Waltham, Massachusetts: Blaisdell Publishing Company, 1968.

INSTRUMENTATION OF THE TAXONOMY OF EDUCATIONAL OBJECTIVES: COGNITIVE DOMAIN

axonomy Classification	Examples of Infinitives	Key Words Examples of Direct Objects
.00 Application	to apply, to generalize, to relate, to choose, to develop, to organize, to use, to employ, to transfer, to restructure, to classify	principles, laws, conclusions, effects, methods, theories, abstractions, situations, generalizations, processes, phenomena, procedures
4.00 Analysis		
4.10 Analysis of Elements	to distinguish, to detect, to identify, to classify, to discriminate, to recognize, to categorize, to deduce	elements, hypothesis/ hypotheses, conclusions, assumptions, statements (of fact), statements (of intent), arguments, particulars
4.20 Analysis of Relationships	to analyze, to contrast, to compare, to distinguish, to deduce	relationships, interrelations, relevance, relevancies, themes, evidence, fallacies, arguments, cause-effect(s), consistency/consistencies, parts, ideas, assumptions
4.30 Analysis of Organizational Principles	to analyze, to distinguish, to detect, to deduce	form(s), pattern(s), purpose(s), point(s) of view, techniques, bias(es), structure(s), theme(s), arrangement(s), organization(s)

INSTRUMENTATION OF THE TAXONOMY OF EDUCATIONAL OBJECTIVES: COGNITIVE DOMAIN

Taxonomy Classification	*Key Words* Examples of Infinitives	Examples of Direct Objects
5.00 Synthesis		
5.10 Production of a Unique Communication	to write, to tell, to relate, to produce, to constitute, to transmit, to originate, to modify, to document	structure(s), pattern(s), product(s), performance(s), design(s), work(s), communications, effort(s), specifics, composition(s)
5.20 Productions of a Plan or Proposed Set of Operations	to propose, to plan, to produce, to design, to modify, to specify	plan(s), objectives, specification(s), schematic(s), operations, way(s), solution(s), means
5.30 Derivation of a Set of Abstraction Relations	to produce, to derive, to develop, to combine, to organize, to synthesize, to classify, to deduce, to develop, to formulate, to modify	phenomena, taxonomies, concept(s), scheme(s), theories, relationships, abstractions, generalizations, hypothesis/hypotheses, perceptions, ways, discoveries
6.00 Evaluation		
6.10 Judgments in Terms of Internal Evidence	to judge, to argue, to validate, to assess, to decide	accuracy/accuracies, consistency/consistencies, fallacies, reliability, flaws, errors, precision, exactness
6.20 Judgments in Terms of External Criteria	to judge, to argue, to consider, to compare, to contrast, to standardize, to appraise	ends, means, efficiency, economy/economies, utility, alternatives, courses of action, standards, theories, generalizations